A.D.D. LAND
The Gift of ADD

By Justine Ruotolo
a.k.a. Miss ADD

A.D.D. Land The Gift of ADD By Justine Marie Ruotolo
ISBN-13: 978-0615882116
ISBN-10: 0615882110
First printing, November 2013
Flying Chickadee
PO Box 30021, Seattle, WA 98113-0021 www.flyingchickadee.com
©2013
Cover design by Michael Gewehr.
Photographs on page 28, 66 and 90 purchased and licensed for print use from shutterstock.com.
Photographs on page 86 by Kenjiko Ono, Elaine Thompson, and Dinesh Korde, respectively.
Photographs on page 88 and 89 by Alexis Tassone.
Photograph on page 90 by Bekah Richards.
Images on page 92, 93 by Gazelle Samizay.
Photograph on page 97 by Stephen Craig Aristei.

2013

This book is dedicated to my parents, George Ruotolo (deceased) and Sophie Ruotolo. Thank you for the gift of life! You taught me to always follow my passion.

To my sons, Christopher and Michael Gewehr. You are the genesis of "The Gift of ADD." Thank you for your encouragement and for helping me stay focused on my dreams. And, to my husband, Stephen Craig Aristei. Thank you for showing me the real meaning of love, and for your continued support as I help others. I love you all, and without you, all of this would mean nothing.

Contents

Preface

Consider the award winning campaign "Think Different" by Steve Jobs and Apple.

> Here's to the crazy ones.
> The misfits. The rebels. The troublemakers.
> The round pegs in the square holes.
> The ones who see things differently.
> They're not fond of rules. And they have no respect for the status quo.
> You can quote them, disagree with them, glorify or vilify them.
> About the only thing you can't do is ignore them.
> Because they change things.
> They invent. They imagine. They heal. They explore. They create. They inspire.
> They push the human race forward.
> Maybe they have to be crazy.
> How else can you stare at an empty canvas and see a work of art?
> Or sit in silence and hear a song that's never been written?
> Or gaze at a red planet and see a laboratory on wheels?
> While some see them as the crazy ones, we see genius.
> Because the people who are crazy enough to think they can change the world,
> are the ones who do.
> © Apple "Think Different" Campaign

If you have ADD, it is more than likely you just saw yourself in the lines above. They capture the often overlooked qualities of ADD, which can be a "gift" for all those blessed with it!

There are two types of Attention Deficit Disorder. Those with ADD Inattentive have a creative mindset and their creative thoughts impair their ability to focus. Children, adolescents and adults with this type of ADD usually go undiagnosed because they fly under the radar. In the school setting, they are often not seen as having a behavior problem. Those with ADHD (Attention Deficit Hyperactivity Disorder) are hyperactive and impulsive. They are usually diagnosed earlier and in school, and like myself, get into trouble. Over the years, ADD has become synonymous with both types of disorders, and you will see both terms used interchangeably throughout this book.

I decided to assemble this book because of the negative labeling and stereotypes that society has attached to the members of the ADHD population: lazy, stupid, absent minded, impulsive, etc...the list goes on and on. None of these labels addresses or describes the real issues of the disorder, yet all of them wholesale undermine one's innate value and the opportunity to maintain a healthy and positive self-esteem, and therefore limit one's ability to live a creative and productive life.

What society as well as most people who suffer from one or more of the many forms of ADHD don't realize or recognize, are the levels of imagination and creativity that come along with having ADHD. People with ADHD are fun, non-linear, out-of-the box thinkers. We make up the majority of the artists, innovators, creators and entrepreneurs of the world.

Very often, the children, adolescents and adults I work with have been beaten down by society and their inability to control the negative aspects of ADHD, which has run unchecked throughout their lives. Many have little or no self-esteem. And many have nearly lost all hope.

If you have ADD, rather than allow all the old stereotypes to box you in, undermine your self-esteem, and rob you of hope, consider how you can acknowledge and embrace your unique gifts! Even beyond teaching the ADHD population how to control and manage the negative aspects of ADHD, and develop the positive aspects, what I truly want you to learn through this book is that ADHD is a gift. I want you to discover your passion in life and connect with your true calling.

As a member of the ADHD population, I want you to see examples of successful ADHD people; people who may have suffered in every way you may have, and yet overcome the obstacles and achieved success and sometimes "greatness." I want you to be encouraged and maybe even find a mentor--someone "just like me," someone who has suffered "just like me," endured all the negative labels, "just like me" and worked past them to pursue their passions toward success.

Possibly the most important observation I made while compiling this book is that in most cases, the people featured found, developed and created their success because of their ADHD, not in spite of it!
So, I want this ADHD population that I so admire and am so passionate about, to not only see examples of success, but most of all to develop and have faith, with the added belief that you too can seek and find your passion, accomplish your goals, and as many of those listed in this book have done, make your dreams come true.

Yes, it is The Gift of ADD!

Sincerely yours,
Justine Ruotolo
Miss ADD

A portion of the proceeds of this book will be given to CHADD (Children and Adults with ADD), a powerful non-profit spreading the word nationally about ADHD, and to the St. Jude Children's Hospital, for never turning anyone away.

Apple and Think Different are registered trademarks of Apple, Inc.

Introduction

I would bet that there are many of you who do not know that ADD is a GIFT!
My name is Justine Ruotolo, and I am also known as Miss ADD. I have been an ADHD/Life Coach for over twenty years. I am also a Marriage and Family Therapist Intern, under the supervision of Ellen Kimmel at the DAZ Foundation. Above all, I am a parent.
I was diagnosed with ADHD when I was forty years old and my two sons, ages twenty-six and twenty-two, also have ADHD.

Initially, after being diagnosed, I lived in fear, not only for myself but also for my oldest son, Chris Gewehr, who was nine at the time. Through the years I have experienced firsthand what many of my clients have shared with me: intense fear, which prevents us from moving forward and discovering our creative mindset. This fear stems from the not so-user-friendly symptoms, which are highlighted during and after the initial diagnosis. These negative symptoms include difficulty focusing and regulating emotions, inattention, hyperactivity, impulsivity, poor communication and social skills, procrastination, and difficulty in relationships.

In my practice I work with children, adolescents, adults, parents, and couples, approaching their ADHD as positive potential, and as a gift! In my quest to help others, I had to learn how to embrace my own ADHD by learning the skillset necessary to manage the negative symptoms, rather than let these symptoms control me. As my own transformation unfolded, I was able to accept ADHD as the greatest gift of my life. I began to see firsthand the positive qualities and opportunities of ADHD, and I was able to see my own creativity—life became fun! The positive qualities are what make us unique, and put us in the category of gifted. People with ADHD are often highly creative, extremely intelligent, determined, energetic, fun-loving, out-of-the box thinkers, passionate, multi-taskers, charming, successful, compassionate, empathetic and hyper-focused, to name a handful of the positive qualities.

Although I do not personally know all the people highlighted in this book, one can enjoy the successes in their life trajectories. One can easily imagine that they also worked through their own fears, learning how to embrace their 'symptoms' and moving past to discover their creativity. I am sure that many struggled with the negative symptoms of ADHD, but they have been able to push through and reach their dreams.

I have told many of my clients that the famous Hollywood sign should really say "ADD Land"! My belief is that there would be no Hollywood were it not for the Gift of ADD; hence, the front cover of this book, designed by my very creative son, Michael Gewehr. He is a student at The Academy of Art University in San Francisco, California. Mike is majoring in Music Production and Sound Design for Visual Media. Because he has found

his passion, his fear is gone, and he is excelling in whatever he does.
I hope that all of you experiencing this book, especially the parents of children and adolescents with ADD, will come to the same realization that I have: ADD is a Gift!

Justine Ruotolo
a.k.a
Miss ADD

A.D.D. LAND

The Gift of ADD

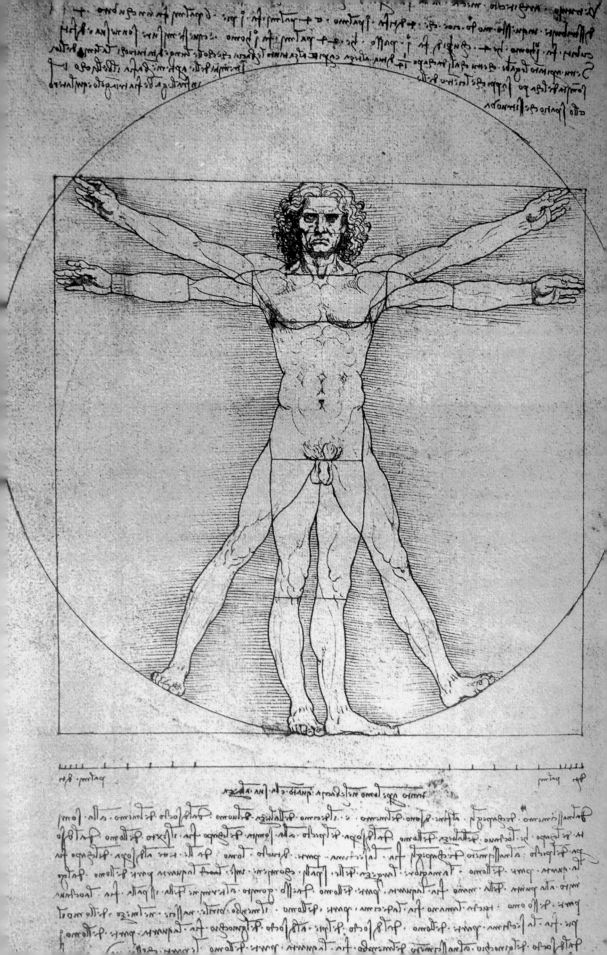

creative

hyperfocused

gifted

Artists and Architects

visualizers

passionate

resourceful

revolutionary

problem solvers

Ansel Adams

American photographer known for his black-and-white photographs of the American West.

Large format camera. © Jose Gil.

Chuck Close

American painter and photographer known for his large-scale photo realist portraits.

Chuck Close, 2008. © lev radin / Shutterstock.com.

Salvador Dalí

Spanish surrealist painter.

Portrait of Picasso, 1947, by Dali. © LUCARELLI TEMISTOCLE / Shutterstock.com.

Walt Disney

American cartoonist, film producer and theme park innovator. When he was a young man working for a newspaper, his editor fired him because he had "no good ideas"!

Disney characters. © s_bukley / Shutterstock.com.

Pablo Picasso

Spanish painter. Known as one of the masters of the twentieth century.

Pablo Picasso, Child with a Dove, *1901. © Neveshkin Nikolay / Shutterstock.com.*

Robert Rauschenberg

American painter and graphic artist.

© Karramba Production.

August Rodin

French sculptor.

August Rodin, The Thinker, *1879-1889. © S1001.*

Richard Rogers

Renowned British architect.

Lloyds building, London. © Christopher Penler.

Vincent van Gogh

Dutch post-Impressionist painter.

Vincent van Gogh, Café Terrace at Night, *1888. © StampGirl / Shutterstock.com.*

Leonardo da Vinci

Famous for his paintings. He was an Italian architect, musician, anatomist, inventor, engineer, sculptor and geometer.

Leonardo da Vinci, Mona Lisa, *c. 2503-1519. © catwalker / Shutterstock.com.*

Frank Lloyd Wright

World renowned, award winning innovator of architectural design.

Ceiling of Guggenheim Museum, New York. © Entropia, LLC / Shutterstock.com.

The artist who is fearful freezes their creative mindset! Mindfulness replaces fear with peace and focus.

~Miss ADD

MUHAMMAD ALI

125

AUSTRIA

C. FREI 2006

BOXING LEGEND

determined

successful

inspirational

Athletes

high-energy

coordinated

team-players

Muhammad Ali

Professional American boxer.

Muhammad Ali, 2004. © Featureflash / Shutterstock.com.

Billy Blanks

An American martial artist, actor and the inventor of Tae Bo.

Billy Blanks, 2011. © DFree / Shutterstock.com.

Scott Eyre

Former left-handed pitcher in Major League Baseball.

Scott Eyre, 2009. © Aspen Photo / Shutterstock.com.

Justin Gatlin

American sprinter and Olympic gold medalist.

Justin Gatlin, 2012. © Ira Bostic / Shutterstock.com.

Duncan Goodhew

Olympic swimmer for Great Britain, winning gold and bronze medals at the 1980 Summer Olympics in Moscow.

Duncan Goodhew, 2012. © Featureflash / Shutterstock.com.

Cammi Granato

Retired American female ice hockey player and one of the first women to be inducted into the Hockey Hall of Fame.

© B Calkins

Tim "Lumpy" Herron

American professional golfer.

Tim Herron, 2008. © Jeff Schultes / Shutterstock.com.

Bruce Jenner

Former US track and field athlete and Olympic gold medalist.

Bruce Jenner. © CarlaVanWagoner / Shutterstock.com.

Magic Johnson

Retired American professional basketball player who played for the LA Lakers in the NBA.

Magic Johnson. © stocklight / Shutterstock.com.

Michael Jordan

Former American professional basketball player who played for the Chicago Bulls in the NBA.

© S.Pytel.

Chris Kaman

German-American professional basketball player for the NBA.

© melis.

Jason Kidd

American professional basketball player for the NBA.

Jason Kidd. © Elias H. Debbas II / Shutterstock.com.

Hank Kuehne

Former American professional golfer.

© Lucky Business.

Frederick Carlton "Carl" Lewis

American former track and field athlete and United Nations Ambassador, who won ten Olympic medals and ten World Championship medals.

Carl Lewis, 2006. © s_bukley / Shutterstock.com.

Vince Lombardi

American former football coach, enshrined in the NFL's Pro Football Hall of Fame in 1971.

Statue of Vince Lombardi, Lambeau Field, Green Bay, WI. © Ffooter / Shutterstock.com.

Greg Louganis

American Olympic diver and author who won two Olympic gold medals.

Greg Louganis, 2010. © s_bukley / Shutterstock.com.

John E. Morgan

English professional golfer.

© Tony Bowler.

Matt Morgan

American professional wrestler and actor.

© max blain / Shutterstock.com.

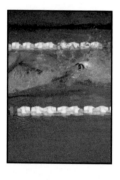

Michael Phelps

Michaels' mother described her son's ADHD symptoms as "classic" - not being able to sit still, constantly tapping his foot, and the inability to focus. She credits the continuous praise and positive reinforcement he received with helping him overcome obstacles and channel his efforts, energies and attention into his passion for swimming, which resulted in his taking home the Olympic gold!

Phelps competing at the Austin Grand Prix, 2012. © Geoff Nelson / Shutterstock.com.

Sir Stephen Geoffrey Redgrave, CBE

Retired British rower who won six Olympic medals.

© Danshutter.

Pete Rose

Former Major League Baseball player and manager.

Pete Rose, 2010. © Helga Esteb / Shutterstock.com.

Babe Ruth

American former Major League Baseball player.

© 9246263575 / Shutterstock.com.

Nolan Ryan

Former Major League Baseball pitcher and owner, and president and CEO of the Texas Rangers.

Texas Rangers. © Aun-Juli Riddle / Shutterstock.com.

Jim Shea Jr.

Retired American skeleton racer and Olympic gold medal winner.

© nikkytok.

Jackie Stewart

Former racing driver from Scottland.

Jackie Stewart, 2009. © Christoff / Shutterstock.com.

Alberto Tomba

Former World Cup alpine ski racer from Italy and Olympic gold medalist.

Alberto Tomba, 2012. © B.Stefanov / Shutterstock.com.

Athletes who have ADD possess the ability to visualize winning the race. This talent, coupled with their determination, is what makes them successful.

~Miss ADD

highly

intelligent

resourceful

Entrepreneurs

determined

out-of-the-box thinkers

courageous

leaders

Sir Richard Branson

Psychology Today reported that people with ADHD are 300% more likely to start their own company, and Sir Richard Branson is living proof, as the founder of the Virgin Group of more than 400 companies. He started his own magazine, *Student*, when he was just sixteen years old.

Sir Richard Branson. © Helga Esteb / Shutterstock.com.

Erin Brokovich-Ellis

American legal clerk and environmental activist who, despite the lack of a formal law school education, was instrumental in constructing a case against the Pacific Gas and Electric Company (PG&E) of California in 1993.

© Africa Studio.

Andrew Carnegie

Scottish-American industrialist who led the expansion of the American steel industry in the late 19th century.

Statue of Andrew Carnegie. © jean morrison.

John T. Chambers

Chairman of the Board and CEO of Cisco Systems, Inc.

Cisco logo. © Adriano Castelli / Shutterstock.com.

Ari Emanuel

American talent agent and co-CEO of William Morris Endeavor (WME), the largest and oldest global talent agency.

© Real Deal Photo.

Malcolm Forbes

Publisher of *Forbes* magazine.

© Cyril Hou.

Henry Ford

Though mostly known as an automobile inventor, Ford really invented and created the first "Production Line," and in doing so, created the first "Affordable Automobile."

Henry Ford. © rook76 / Shutterstock.com.

Bill Gates

Co-founder of Microsoft and philanthropist.

Bill Gates. © 3777190317 / Shutterstock.com.

William Randolph Hearst

American newspaper publisher who built the nation's largest newspaper chain.

Hearst Castle, San Simeon, CA. © Dan Schreiber.

Milton Hershey

Founder of the Hershey Chocolate Company.

Hershey's Kiss. © Christopher S. Howeth.

Tommy Hilfiger

American fashion designer and founder of the brand Tommy Hilfiger Corporation.

Tommy Hilfiger, 2007. © stocklight / Shutterstock.com.

Howard Hughes

American business man, aviator, aerospace engineer, filmmaker and philanthropist.

© Ensuper.

Steve Jobs

Co-founder of Apple Inc. and Pixar Animation Studios.

Apple store, New York. © Andrey Bayda / Shutterstock.com.

Ingvar Kamprad

Founder of IKEA.

IKEA store, Beijing, China. © testing / Shutterstock.com.

David Neeleman

David Neeleman credits his success and creation of JetBlue to his ADHD because "with the disorder comes creativity and the ability to always think 'outside the box'"! He has reported that his ADHD prevents him from being detail-oriented, stating, "I have an easier time planning a 20-aircraft fleet than I do paying the light bill."

© Jeff Schultes / Shutterstock.com.

Paul Orfalea

Paul Orfalea's dyslexia and extreme ADD may have caused him to flunk second grade and earn Cs and Ds in college, but he credits ADD with helping him start the copy chain Kinko's (named after his nickname, due to his ADD and curly hair). Paul also believes his ADHD is a "gift" because it "lets him think big without getting weighed down by details"!

© Glovatskiy.

H. Ross Perot

Founder of Electronic Data Systems and Perot Systems. He also ran for President of the United States in 1992 and 1996.

US Capitol Building, Washington DC. © Orhan Cam.

John D. Rockefeller

American industrialist and philanthropist who founded Standard Oil Company.

Rockefeller Center, New York. © SeanPavonePhoto / Shutterstock.com.

Ted Turner

Founder of CNN, the first 24-hour cable news channel.

Ted Turner, 2004. © Featureflash / Shutterstock.com.

F.W. Woolworth

Founder of F.W. Woolworth Company, now Foot Locker.

Foot Locker store in Copenhagen, Denmark. © Tupungato / Shutterstock.com.

William Wrigley Jr.

US chewing gum industrialist who founded Wrigley Jr. Company.

© Africa Studio.

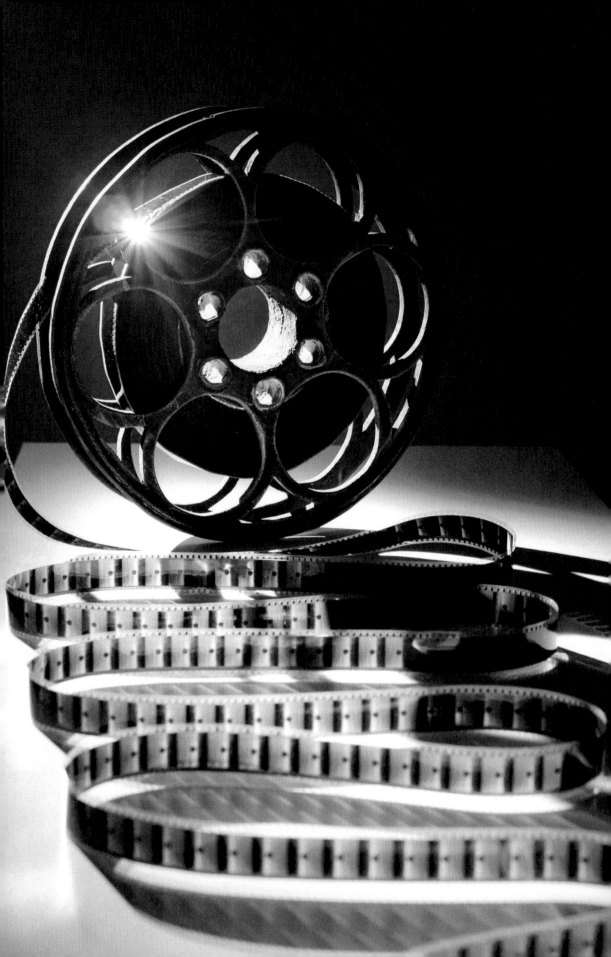

charismatic

gifted fun-loving

Entertainers

creative

passionate

versatile

charming

Harry Anderson

American actor and magician.

Harry Anderson, 2010. © Helga Esteb / Shutterstock.com.

Anne Bancroft

American actress associated with the method acting school. She won one Academy Award, three BAFTA Awards, two Golden Globes, two Tony Awards and two Emmy Awards.

Anne Bancroft, 1990. © David Fowler / Shutterstock.com.

Glenn Beck

American conservative, television network producer, radio host, author, entrepreneur, and political commentator. He hosts the *Glenn Beck Program*.

Glenn Beck, 2011. © s_bukley / Shutterstock.com.

Orlando Bloom

English actor who had his breakthrough role in *Lord of the Rings*.

Orlando Bloom, 2002. © Featureflash / Shutterstock.com.

George Burns

American comedian, actor, and writer.

George Burns, 2009. © Jaguar PS / Shutterstock.com.

Jim Carrey

Canadian American actor, comedian, and producer and winner of two Golden Globe Awards.

Jim Carrey. © Featureflash / Shutterstock.com.

Jennifer Connelly

American film actress.

Jennifer Connelly, 2001. © Featureflash / Shutterstock.com.

Anderson Cooper

American journalist, author, and television personality. He is the primary anchor of the CNN news show *Anderson Cooper 360°*.

Anderson Cooper, 2011. © DFree / Shutterstock.com.

Bill Cosby

American comedian, actor, author, television producer, educator, musician and activist.

Bill Cosby, 1997. © Featureflash / Shutterstock.com.

Patrick Dempsey

American actor best known for his role on the show *Grey's Anatomy.*

Patrick Dempsey, 2007. © s_bukley / Shutterstock.com.

Zooey Deschanel

American actress, musician, and singer-songwriter.

Zooey Deschanel, 2012. © Helga Esteb / Shutterstock.com.

Robert De Niro

American actor, director and producer and Academy Award winner.

Robert De Niro, 2011. © cinemafestival. / Shutterstock.com.

Kirk Douglas

American stage and film actor, film producer and author.

Kirk Douglas, 1999. © Featureflash / Shutterstock.com.

Patty Duke

American actress of stage, film, and television and winner of an Academy Award at age 16.

© kanate.

Rick Fox

Canadian television actor and retired professional basketball player who last played for the NBA's Los Angeles Lakers in 2004.

Rick Fox, 2008. © s_bukley / Shutterstock.com.

Danny Glover

American actor, film director and political activist.

Danny Glover. © Vinicius Tupinamba.

Brian Grazer

American film and television producer. His films and TV shows have been nominated for 43 Academy Awards, and 131 Emmys.

Brian Grazer, 2001. © Featureflash / Shutterstock.com.

Tracey Gold

American actress and former child star best known for playing Carol Seaver on the sitcom *Growing Pains*.

Tracey Gold, 2012. © lev radin / Shutterstock.com.

Whoopi Goldberg

American comedian, actress, singer-songwriter, political activist, author and talk show host.

Whoopi Goldberg, 2000. © Featureflash / Shutterstock.com.

Woody Harrelson

American actor whose breakout role was in the sitcom *Cheers*.

Woody Harrelson, 2012. © DFree / Shutterstock.com.

Melissa Joan Hart

American actor, writer, television director, television producer, singer and businesswoman.

Melissa Joan Hart, 2010. © DFree / Shutterstock.com.

Mariette Hartley

American actress and Emmy Award winner.

Mariette Hartley, 2010. © Helga Esteb / Shutterstock.com.

Salma Hayek

Mexican American film actress, director and producer.

Salma Hayek, 2010. © s_bukley / Shutterstock.com.

Mariel Hemingway

American actress and paternal granddaughter of writer Ernest Hemingway.

Mariel Hemingway, 2007. © s_bukley / Shutterstock.com.

Alfred Hitchcock

English film director and producer.

Alfred Hitchcock featured on a US stamp. © Neftali / Shutterstock.com.

Dustin Hoffman

American actor with a career in film, television, and theatre. Hoffman has won two Academy Awards, five Golden Globes, four BAFTAs, three Drama Desk Awards, a Genie Award, and an Emmy Award. He received the AFI Life Achievement Award in 1999, and the Kennedy Center Honors in 2012.

Dustin Hoffman, 1997. © Featureflash / Shutterstock.com.

Anthony Hopkins

Welsh actor of film, stage, and television, and a composer. In addition to his Academy Award, Hopkins has also won three BAFTA Awards, two Emmys and a Golden Globe Award. Hopkins was knighted by Queen Elizabeth II in 1993 for services to the arts.

Anthony Hopkins, 2011. © s_bukley / Shutterstock.com.

Eddie Izzard

British stand-up comedian, actor and writer.

Eddie Izzard, 2012. © Featureflash / Shutterstock.com.

Evel Knievel

American daredevil and painter. He was inducted into the Motorcycle Hall of Fame in 1999.

© Planner. / Shutterstock.com.

Christopher Knight

American actor best known for playing Peter Brady on the 1970s series, *The Brady Bunch*.

Christopher Knight, 2008. © s_bukley / Shutterstock.com.

Jay Leno

American stand-up comedian and television host.

Jay Leno, 2004. © Featureflash / Shutterstock.com.

Brad Little

American musical theatre actor and winner of a Barrymore Award. In 1994 he joined the cast of *The Phantom of the Opera*.

© Scott Rothstein.

Howie Mandel

Canadian comedian, actor, and television host. He is well known as host of the game show *Deal or No Deal*.

Howie Mandel, 2011. © Helga Esteb / Shutterstock.com.

Patrick McKenna

Canadian comedian and actor best known for his role in *The Red Green Show*.

© Anton Prado PHOTO.

Steve McQueen

American actor and highest-paid movie star in the world in 1974.

Steve McQueen, 2009. © Jaguar PS / Shutterstock.com.

Jack Nicholson

American actor, film director, producer, writer and three-time Academy Award winner.

Jack Nicholson, 1998. © Featureflash / Shutterstock.com.

Roxy Olin

American actress in the show *Brothers and Sisters*. When she was young, Roxy earned the nicknamed "Rollover," because she did somersaults, nonstop, around the house.

Roxy Olin, 2010. © Helga Esteb / Shutterstock.com.

Edward James Olmos

Mexican American actor and director nominated for an Academy Award in 1988.

Edward James Olmos, 2008. © s_bukley / Shutterstock.com.

Joe Pantoliano

American film and television actor who has played roles in *The Sopranos*, *The Matrix* and *Memento*.

Joe Pantoliano, 2010. © Charles Edwards / Shutterstock.com.

Theo Paphitis

British entrepreneur who is known for his appearances on the BBC business program *Dragon's Den*.

Theo Paphitis, 2012. © Featureflash / Shutterstock.com.

Dan Rather

American journalist and the former news anchor for the *CBS Evening News*.

Dan Rather, 2003. © Featureflash / Shutterstock.com.

Guy Ritchie

English screenwriter, film director and producer.

Guy Ritchie, 2011. © s_bukley / Shutterstock.com.

Joan Rivers

American television personality, comedian, writer, film director, and actress.

Joan Rivers, 2003. © Featureflash / Shutterstock.com.

Michelle Rodriguez

American actress whose breakout role was in the film *Girlfight*.

Michelle Rodriguez, 2011. © Photo Works / Shutterstock.com.

George C. Scott

American stage and film actor, director and producer well known for his portrayal of General George S. Patton in the film *Patton*.

© James Steidl.

Karina Smirnoff

Ukrainian professional ballroom dancer. She is best known to the general public as a professional dancer on *Dancing with the Stars*.

Karina Smirnoff, 2011. © s_bukley / Shutterstock.com.

Tom Smothers

American comedian, composer and musician, best known as half of the musical comedy team, The Smothers Brothers, alongside his younger brother Dick.

Tom Smothers, 2008. © s_bukley / Shutterstock.com.

Suzanne Somers

American actress, author, singer and businesswoman, known for her television role on *Three's Company*.

Suzanne Somers, 2008. © s_bukley / Shutterstock.com.

Steven Spielberg

American film director, screenwriter, producer, and studio entrepreneur. Upon entering Long Beach State College, he was told by his film instructor, to "go find some other area to pursue, because he would never become a successful director."

Steven Spielberg, 2011. © CarlaVanWagoner.

Sylvester Stallone

American actor, filmmaker, screenwriter and film director.

Sylvester Stallone, 1998. © Featureflash / Shutterstock.com.

James Stewart

American film and stage actor.

James Stewart as featured on a US stamp. © Neftali / Shutterstock.com.

Trudie Styler

English actress and producer.

Trudie Styler, 2007. © s_bukley / Shutterstock.com.

Liv Tyler

American actress and model.

Liv Tyler, 2002. © Featureflash / Shutterstock.com.

Vince Vaughn

American film actor, screenwriter, producer, comedian and activist.

Vince Vaughn, 2011. © s_bukley / Shutterstock.com.

Lindsey Wagner

American actress who won an Emmy Award for her role in the television series *The Bionic Woman*.

© Joe Seer. / Shutterstock.com.

Mike Wallace

American journalist, game show host, actor and media personality. He was one of the original correspondents for CBS' *60 Minutes*.

© Mike Flippo.

Emma Watson

English actress and model who rose to prominence playing Hermione Granger in the *Harry Potter* films.

Emma Watson, 2012. © s_bukley / Shutterstock.com.

Henry Winkler

American actor, director, producer and author best known for his role as Fonzie on the 1970s sitcom *Happy Days*.

Henry Winkler, 2007. © s_bukley / Shutterstock.com.

Robin Williams

American actor and comedian.

Robin Williams, 2011. © s_bukley / Shutterstock.com.

The entertainer who has
ADD is at home in ADD Land.
Here, they feel understood
because their creative mindset is
shared by everyone!

~Miss ADD

charismatic

ingenious

creative

Musicians

powerful

talented

expressive

inspiring

Daniel Bedingfield

New Zealand born British singer-songwriter. In 2004, Bedingfield won a BRIT Award for Best British Male Artist.

Daniel Bedingfield, 2011. © Helga Esteb / Shutterstock.com.

Ludwig van Beethoven

German composer and pianist.

Ludwig van Beethoven. © Nicku Shutterstock.com.

Harry Belafonte Jr.

American singer, songwriter, actor and social activist. He is perhaps best known for singing "The Banana Boat Song," with its catchy lyric, "Day-O".

Harry Belafonte Jr., 2011. © cinemafestival. / Shutterstock.com.

Tony Bennett

Italian-American singer of popular music, standards, show tunes, and jazz.

Tony Bennett, 1999. © Featureflash / Shutterstock.com.

Cher

American singer and actress.

Cher, 2000. © Featureflash / Shutterstock.com.

Kurt Cobain

American musician and artist, best known as the lead singer of the band Nirvana.

© mffoto.

Brandon Curtis

Vocalist, bassist and keyboardist for the band *The Secret Machines*.

© Sinelyov.

John Denver

American singer/songwriter, activist, and humanitarian. He had twelve gold and four platinum albums.

John Denver. © Steve Broer / Shutterstock.com.

Hillary Duff

American actress, singer, songwriter, entrepreneur, author, and humanitarian.

Hillary Duff, 2003. © Featureflash / Shutterstock.com.

Jon Finn

American rock musician and guitarist. He is the founder and leader of the *Jon Finn Group*, and is a professor at the Berklee College of Music.

© Sinelyov.

Noel Gallagher

English musician, singer and songwriter and principal songwriter of the band Oasis.

Noel Gallagher, 2011. © Harmony Gerber.

George Frideric Handel

German-born British Baroque composer.

George Handel, Engraved by J.Thomson. © Georgios Kollidas / Shutterstock.com.

Stephan Jenkins

American musician best known as the lead singer, songwriter, and guitarist for *Third Eye Blind*.

Stephan Jenkins, 2000. © Featureflash / Shutterstock.com.

Solange Knowles

American singer-songwriter, actress, model, dancer, and DJ.

Solange Knowles, 2008. © s_bukley / Shutterstock.com.

John Lennon

English musician, songwriter and founding member of *The Beatles*.

John Lennon featured on German stamp. © catwalker / Shutterstock.com.

Adam Levine

American singer-songwriter, musician and occasional actor best known as the front man for the band *Maroon 5*.

Adam Levine, 2011. © s_bukley / Shutterstock.com.

Courtney Love

American singer-songwriter, musician, actress and artist. Love initially gained notoriety as vocalist and rhythm guitarist of the rock band *Hole*.

Courtney Love, 2012. © s_bukley / Shutterstock.com.

Wolfgang Amadeus Mozart

Austrian composer of the Classical era.

Wolfgang Amadeus Mozart. © Nicku / Shutterstock.com.

Cole Porter

American composer and songwriter.

Cole Porter featured on US stamp. © rook76 / Shutterstock.com.

Elvis Presley

American singer and actor.

Elvis Presley, © rook76 / Shutterstock.com.

Sergei Rachmaninoff

Russian composer, pianist and conductor.

© Pelfophoto.

Buddy Rich

American jazz drummer and band leader.

© Telekhovskyi.

Britney Spears

American recording artist and entertainer.

Britney Spears, 1999. © Featureflash / Shutterstock.com.

Joss Stone

English soul singer, songwriter and actress.

Joss Stone, 2012. © Gustavo Miguel Fernandes.

Justin Timberlake

American actor, businessman, and singer-songwriter. Justin Timberlake has both OCD and ADD.

Justin Timberlake, 2010. © Helga Esteb / Shutterstock.com.

Steven Tyler

American singer, songwriter, and multi-instrumentalist, best known as the lead singer of the band Aerosmith.

Steven Tyler, 2002. © TDC Photography.

Bob Weir

American singer, songwriter, and guitarist, most recognized as a founding member of the Grateful Dead.

Bob Weir, 1994. © Northfoto.

Stevie Wonder

American singer, songwriter, and multi-instrumentalist. He has won 22 Grammy Awards and a Grammy Lifetime Achievement Award.

Stevie Wonder, 2012. © Gustavo Miguel Fernandes.

The musician with ADD
ruminates to music in their head.
They can associate anything
they see with a tune!
Hyperfocus is their friend.
~Miss ADD

resilient

inspiring

determined

leaders

Political & Public Figures

charismatic

brave

revolutionary

resourceful

philanthropists

Napoleon Bonaparte

French military and political leader who rose to prominence during the latter stages of the French Revolution.

Painting of Napoleon by L. David. © Pshenichka / Shutterstock.com.

Col. Gregory "Pappy" Boyington

United States Marine Corps officer who was an American fighter ace during World War II.

Boyington's head stone in Arlington Cemetery. © Guy J. Sagi.

George H. W. Bush

41st US President.

George H. W. Bush, 1992. © Steve Broer / Shutterstock.com.

George W. Bush

43rd US President.

George W. Bush, 2006. © Northfoto / Shutterstock.com.

Admiral Richard Byrd

American naval officer who specialized in feats of exploration. He was a pioneering American aviator, polar explorer, and organizer of polar logistics.

Richard Byrd. © Neftali / Shutterstock.com.

James Carville

American political commentator and media personality who is a prominent figure in the Democratic Party.

James Carville, 2011. © s_bukley / Shutterstock.com.

Prince Charles

Prince of Wales.

Prince Charles, 2012. © S.K Photography / Shutterstock.com.

Sir Winston Churchill

British politician, best known for his leadership of the United Kingdom during the Second World War. He was also a historian, writer, and artist. He is the only British Prime Minister to have received the Nobel Prize in Literature.

Sir Winston Churchill. © Andy Lidstone / Shutterstock.com.

Dwight D. Eisenhower

34th President of the United States.

Dwight D. Eisenhower. © Olga Popova / Shutterstock.com.

Thomas Jefferson

American Founding Father, the principal author of the Declaration of Independence and the third President of the United States.

Statue of Thomas Jefferson. © Kevin D. Oliver.

John F. Kennedy

35th President of the United States.

John F. Kennedy. © Neftali / Shutterstock.com

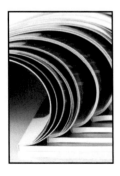

John F. Kennedy Jr.

Elder son of John F. Kennedy, magazine publisher and lawyer.

© Africa Studio.

Robert F. Kennedy

Democratic senator from New York and a noted civil-rights activist.

Robert F. Kennedy. © Keepsmiling4u / Shutterstock.com.

Abraham Lincoln

Though he eventually became the 16th U.S. President, it is a little known fact that upon serving in the military he entered the Black Hawk War as a Captain and came out a Private.

Abraham Lincoln. © thatsmymop.

Gamal Abdel Nasser

Second President of Egypt. He led the Egyptian Revolution of 1952 which overthrew the monarchy of Egypt and Sudan, and heralded a new period of socialist reform in Egypt with a profound advancement of pan-Arab nationalism.

Gamal Abdel Nasser. © rook76 / Shutterstock.com.

Gavin Newsom

American politician who is the 49th and current Lieutenant Governor of California. Previously, he was the 42nd Mayor of San Francisco.

Gavin Newsom, 2009. © amehdiza / Shutterstock.com.

George S. Patton

General in the United States Army during World War II.

George S. Patton. © Tupungato / Shutterstock.com.

Eddie Rickenbacker

American fighter ace in World War I and Medal of Honor recipient.

Eddie Rickenbacker. © vadimmmus / Shutterstock.com.

Nelson Rockefeller

41st Vice President of the United States serving under President Gerald Ford.

© spirit of america / Shutterstock.com.

Anna Eleanor Roosevelt

Longest-serving First Lady of the United States. She also served as the first chair of the UN Commission on Human Rights and oversaw the drafting of the Universal Declaration of Human Rights.

Statue of Anna Eleanor Roosevelt. © Carolyn M Carpenter.

Anwar al-Sadat

Third President of Egypt. He won the Nobel Peace Prize for his negotiations with Israel, which culminated in the Egypt–Israel Peace Treaty.

Anwar al-Sadat. © rook76 / Shutterstock.com.

Norman Schwarzkopf

United States Army general during the Persian Gulf War.

Schwarzkopf leads Desert Storm parade, 1991. © spirit of america / Shutterstock.com.

George Washington

One of the Founding Fathers of the United States and the first American President.

Washington. Engraved by W. Humphreys. © Georgios Kollidas / Shutterstock.com.

William Westmoreland

United States Army General who commanded US military operations in the Vietnam War at its peak, during the Tet Offensive.

© Kletr.

Woodrow Wilson

28th President of the United States. He was awarded the 1919 Nobel Peace Prize for his sponsorship of the League of Nations.

Woodrow Wilson. © Boris15 / Shutterstock.com.

Political leaders with ADD
are grandiose and charismatic,
which helps them captivate
their audience.

~Miss ADD

adventurous

out-of-the-box

thinkers

Scientists and Explorers

courageous

determined

trend-setters

creative

Alexander Graham Bell

Scientist, inventor, engineer and innovator credited with inventing the first practical telephone.

© Mike Flippo.

Werner Von Braun

German-American rocket scientist, aerospace engineer, and space architect. He is credited as being the "Father of Rocket Science." He led the development of the Saturn V booster rocket that helped land the first men on the Moon.

Saturn V rocket thrusters. © mgen27 / Shutterstock.com.

Wright Brothers

American brothers, inventors, and aviation pioneers credited with inventing and building the world's first successful airplane.

© Elenarts.

Sir Richard Francis Burton

British geographer, explorer, translator, writer, cartographer, ethnologist, linguist, fencer and diplomat. According to one count, he spoke twenty-nine European, Asian and African languages.

© Daniele Pietrobelli.

Christopher Columbus

Spanish explorer, navigator and colonizer. His four voyages across the Atlantic Ocean led to the Spanish colonization of the New World.

Christopher Columbus. © Georgios Kollidas / Shutterstock.com.

Harvey Cushing, M.D.

A pioneer of brain surgery, he was the first person to describe Cushing's syndrome. He is often called the "father of modern neurosurgery."

Harvey Cushing. © Solodov Alexey / Shutterstock.com.

Thomas Edison

American inventor and businessman who developed many devices, including the phonograph, the motion picture camera, and a long-lasting electric light bulb. Considered one of the most prolific inventors, holding a record of 1,093 patents in his name, when he was young, his teachers told him that he was "too stupid to learn anything."

© Sergey Nivens.

Albert Einstein

German-born theoretical physicist who developed the general theory of relativity, one of the two pillars of modern physics. He was four years old before he could speak and seven before he could read.

Albert Einstein. © YANGCHAO / Shutterstock.com.

Michael Faraday

English physicist and chemist whose many experiments contributed greatly to the understanding of electromagnetism.

Michael Faraday, engraved by J. Cochran. © Georgios Kollidas / Shutterstock.com.

Benjamin Franklin

Founding Father of the United States, scientist and inventor. He invented the lightning rod and bifocals among other things.

© szpeti.

Galileo Galilei

Italian physicist, mathematician, astronomer, and philosopher who played a major role in the Scientific Revolution. His achievements include improvements to the telescope and astronomical observations.

Galileo Galilei. © Iryna1 / Shutterstock.com.

Stephen Hawking

British theoretical physicist, cosmologist, and author.

© arindambanerjee / Shutterstock.com.

Meriwether Lewis

American explorer, soldier, and public administrator, best known for his role as the leader of the Lewis and Clark Expedition with William Clark.

Lewiston, ID, named after Meriwether Lewis. © Bill Perry.

James Clerk Maxwell

Scottish physicist best known for his formulation of electromagnetic theory.

James Clerk Maxwell. © Nicku.

Isaac Newton

English physicist, mathematician, astronomer, natural philosopher, alchemist and theologian. He made important theories on calculus, optics and the law of gravitation.

© BMJ.

Nostradamus

French astrologer and physician, the most widely read seer of the Renaissance.

Sculpture of Nostradamus. © mtsyri.

Louis Pasteur

French chemist and microbiologist who created the first vaccines for rabies and anthrax. He also created pasteurization, a method to treat wine and milk to prevent sickness.

© Efired.

Socrates

Greek philosopher who had a profound influence on ancient and modern philosophy.

Statue of Socrates, Athens, Greece. © stefanel.

Nikola Tesla

Serbian-American inventor, electrical engineer, mechanical engineer, and physicist best known for his contributions to the design of the modern alternating current (AC) electrical supply system.

Tesla coil. © jcjgphotography.

Scientists with ADD are able
to see the similarities in polar
opposites. Their creativity leads to
important discoveries.

~Miss ADD

imaginative

communicators

adventurous

Writers

creative

expressive

intelligent

entertaining

teachers

Scott Adams

Creator of the *Dilbert* comic strip and author of several nonfiction works.

© Refat.

Hans Christian Anderson

Danish author and poet best remembered for his fairy tales.

Statue of Hans Christian Anderson, Copenhagen Denmark. © Alan Kraft.

Robert Benton

American screenwriter, film director and Academy Award winner.

Robert Benton, 2003. © Featureflash / Shutterstock.com.

Charlotte and Emily Brontë

Poets and novelists who originally published their work under masculine pseudonyms. Charlotte Brontë wrote *Jane Eyre*, while Emily Brontë wrote *Wuthering Heights*.

Illustration of Charlotte Bronte from British stamp. © IgorGolovniov / Shutterstock.com.

Lord Byron

English poet and a leading figure in the Romantic movement.

Lord Byron. Engraved by H. Robinson. © Georgios Kollidas / Shutterstock.com.

Stephen J. Cannell

American television producer, writer and novelist.

Stephen J. Cannell, 2006. © Helga Esteb / Shutterstock.com.

Thomas Carlyle

Scottish philosopher, writer, historian and teacher during the Victorian era.

Statue of Thomas Carlyle, Chelsea, London. © BasPhoto.

Lewis Carroll

English writer most famous for *Alice's Adventures in Wonderland*.

Alice's Adventures in Wonderland. *Engraving by John Tenniel. © Oleg Golovnev.*

Agatha Christie

British writer of novels, short stories and plays. Some of her well-known characters are Hercule Poirot, Miss Jane Marple and Tommy and Tuppence.

Orient Express (feat. in Murder on the Orient Express). © *Pres Panayotov / Shutterstock.com.*

Samuel Clemens (Mark Twain)

American author known for *The Adventures of Tom Sawyer* and *Adventures of Huckleberry Finn*.

Tom Sawyer *painted by Norman Rockwell.* © *AlexanderZam*

Gareth Cook

American journalist, editor and Pulitzer Prize winner.

© *malinx.*

Emily Dickinson

American poet whose poems are unique for the era in which she wrote.

US stamp featuring Emily Dickinson. © *Boris15 / Shutterstock.com*

John Dunning

American writer of non-fiction and detective fiction.

© sergign.

Katherine Ellison

Investigative journalist and foreign correspondent who won the Pulitzer Prize for International Reporting.

© wellphoto.

Ralph Waldo Emerson

American essayist and poet.

Ralph Waldo Emerson house. © Zack Frank.

F. Scott Fitzgerald

American author of short stories and novels including *The Great Gatsby*.

US stamp showing Fitzgerald. © Neftali / Shutterstock.com

Gustave Flaubert

French writer counted among the greatest novelists in Western literature.

© Garsya.

Richard Ford

American novelist and short story writer. His novel, *Independence Day*, won both the PEN/Faulkner Award and the Pulitzer Prize for Fiction.

© Zemler.

Robert Frost

American poet who received four Pulitzer Prizes for Poetry.

Robert Frost on US stamp. © Olga Popova / Shutterstock.com.

Terry Goodkind

American author of *The Sword of Truth* series and *The Law of Nines*.

© ouh_desire

John Grisham

American lawyer, politician and author, best known for his popular legal thrillers. Several of his books have been adapted for film.

© TrotzOlga.

Ernest Hemingway

American author and journalist. He won the Nobel Prize in Literature in 1954.

Caricature of Ernest Hemingway. © Boris15 / Shutterstock.com

John Irving

American novelist and Academy Award-winning screenwriter.

John Irving, 2000. © Featureflash / Shutterstock.com.

Dr. Samuel Johnson

English writer who wrote *A Dictionary of the English Language*.

Engraving of Samuel Johnson by W. Holl. © Georgios Kollidas / Shutterstock.com.

Edgar Allan Poe

American author, poet, editor and literary critic.

US stamp featuring Edgar Allan Poe. © Neftali / Shutterstock.com

Philip Schultz

American poet and co-winner of the 2008 Pullitzer Prize in Poetry.

© Graeme Dawes.

George Bernard Shaw

Irish playwright and a co-founder of the London School of Economics.

US stamp featuring George Bernard Shaw. © Kiev.Victor / Shutterstock.com.

Robert Lewis Stevenson

Scottish writer famous for *Treasure Island, Kidnapped* and *Strange Case of Dr. Jekyll and Mr. Hyde.*

© arka38.

Lord Alfred Tennyson

Poet Laureate of Great Britain and Ireland during much of Queen Victoria's reign.

Lord Tennyson. © brandonht / Shutterstock.com.

Henry David Thoreau

American author who is best known for his book *Walden*.

Thoreau featured on a US stamp. © Lefteris Papaulakis / Shutterstock.com.

Leo Tolstoy

Russian writer of novels and short stories. He flunked out of college.

Leo Tolstoy. Picture from Meyers Lexicon Books. © Nicku.

Jules Verne

French author who pioneered the science fiction genre in Europe. He is best known for *Twenty Thousand Leagues Under the Sea*, *Journey to the Center of the Earth* and *Around the World in Eighty Days*.

Jules Verne. © rook76 / Shutterstock.com.

Victor Villaseñor

Victor Villaseñor is an acclaimed Mexican-American writer, best known for the New York Times bestseller novel *Rain of Gold*.

© Geanina Bechea.

Walter Whitman

American poet, essayist and journalist.

Walter Whitman. © rook76 / Shutterstock.com.

Tennessee Williams

An American writer who received the Pulitzer Prize for Drama for *A Streetcar Named Desire* and *Cat on a Hot Tin Roof*.

Tennessee Williams as featured on a US stamp. © Neftali / Shutterstock.com

Sharon Wohlmuth

Prize-winning photographer and co-author of eleven books. She is the only photojournalist to make *The New York Times* bestsellers' list three times.

© Patryk Kosmider.

Virginia Woolf

An English Writer and author of *A Room of One's Own*, among other books.

© Galushko Sergey.

William Butler Yeats

Irish poet and winner of the Nobel Prize in Literature.

Yeats as featured on an Irish stamp. © Brendan Howard / Shutterstock.com.

My Brain on ADD, by Alexis Tassone

musician

writer

filmmaker

painter

Case Studies

chef

composer

photographer

makeup artist

Drawings by Alexis Tassone.

Alexis Tassone

I met Alexis when she was twelve years old. Her wonderful parents hired me because she was struggling in school. Immediately, I recognized her innate abilities in the creative world. Alexis is twenty years old today, and as the years went by, her creativity has blossomed to encompass it all. From freehand drawing, to animé, baking "Tabasco" cupcakes, to cooking elaborate meals, designing and sewing clothes and costumes, to teaching herself how to play piano and ukulele, from photography to making short films and of course her intense interest in make-up, special effects and masks, there appears to be no end to what Alexis won't try. She is presently working as an intern in Hollywood learning the intricacies of prosthesis makeup.

I know that Alexis will successfully move forward in her life, doing what she loves. She has learned to embrace and work with her ADD. She has found her passion, but continues to explore other avenues in her creative mindset. Alexis is fearless, and that is the reason that she is able to explore her passions successfully. I am very proud of who this young woman is, and encourage her always to "Catch her Dreams"!

Makeup and costumes by Alexis Tassone.

Dishes prepared by Alexis Tassone.

Michael W. Gewehr

This highly creative individual is my son. From the time he was nine months old, it was apparent that he had a "Gift." I remember walking into the den and seeing Michael putting his peanut butter and jelly sandwich into the VCR. He was curious about how this machine worked. He watched his father and I put objects into the opening and he wanted to try it for himself. His creativity was apparent from the time he was in elementary school. He had a love for drawing and music. When he was in sixth grade, he decided he wanted to join his middle school orchestra. To my surprise, he came home with the cello. He picked it up quickly, and continued to play it throughout high school. In addition he also played the bass guitar, which he was able to learn on his own. He was part of a live news program at Palos Verdes High School, called *Live From 205*. This was a blessing! Like most children/adolescents with ADD, Mike struggled with the academic part of school. *Live From 205* became his creative connection to his high school. Everyone in the program, had to maintain a C average to continue, and because he loved the program so much, he was able to do this. He learned a lot about the inside of a news program, and was the producer of the show in his senior year. He learned how to videotape, and edit the film that came in for the show.

When he started his college career at The Academy of Art University, it was Illustration that he picked for his major. His love for art was the reason for this, but that soon changed. He began his second semester majoring in Music Production and Sound Design for Visual Media, which he continues today. His love for music is powerful, as is his ability to compose. In addition to cello and bass guitar, Mike also plays the guitar, piano, and the upright bass, and every one of these instruments was self-taught. I believe that Michael's creativity has no boundaries. This is because he has released the fear related to his anxiety. He is able to stay in the moment, which helps him to be in control of his negative ADD symptoms.

Mike did well in high school, but I knew that if I sent him to a state school, he would struggle with the mundane and boring academic subjects. This is why we decided to send him to a school that would embrace his creative mindset. Mike is excelling in college; his grades are high because he found his passion. Mike will be finished with college in a year and a half, and is looking forward to using his education to follow his dream.

My feelings on dating..., *Watercolor & Pen, 8x8," 2013.*   Confronted, *Watercolor & Pencil, 12x12," 2013.*

Bleeding Buddhas, *Watercolor, 8x5," 2013.*

Gazelle Samizay

I met Gazelle shortly after she moved to Los Angeles from Seattle. She had recently been diagnosed with ADD (inattentive) and was seeking coaching to help her manage her diverse interests. As a freelance designer and practicing artist in photography and video, she struggled with balancing her projects from a peaceful place rather than one of stress, since stress is what motivated her to complete projects.

With interests in art, music, and writing, I could see that she was talented and had achieved a great deal of success, but that she was only using a small amount of her creative potential. In order to help her release her fears and unblock her creativity I asked her to draw whenever she felt fearful, down, or any other negative emotion. Drawing was not a medium she had used for over ten years and as a perfectionist, she was tentative about doing something that she did not feel she had mastered.

She approached the drawings in a very intuitive way, without the detailed planning normally ascribed to her photography and video work. She let go of the idea that there was an audience she had to please and just drew and painted whatever came to her mind. As an added step, she decided to post whatever she drew to her Facebook page in order to help her release expectations from others about whether the work was "good" or not.

The result was very surprising for her. She found that this was the first time since she was nine years old that she truly had fun and felt free in creating art. It's not that she didn't enjoy the other projects she had done, but they were always overshadowed with stress and fear that sapped the fun out of the creative process.

This exercise created a tremendous breakthrough for her and as an added benefit, sharing her drawings allowed her to connect with new people and even inspired others to pursue their creative interests.

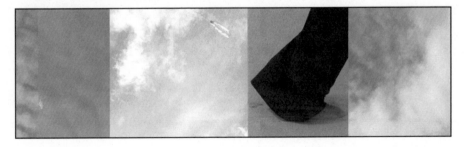

Ravel, Video Still, 7:51, 2012. www.gazellesamizay.com, www.in-visionproductions.

Resources

Parenting.com: 19 Celebrities with ADHD

Attitude Magazine: Famous People With ADHD and Learning Disabilities

ADD About.com: Famous People With ADD/ADHD

Voices.Yahoo.com: Famous People ADD/ADHD – Positive Side Of ADD

ADHDrelief.com: Famous & Notable People With Attention Deficit Disorder

Wikipedia.com: List of People with Attention Deficit Hyperactivity Disorder

ADDAdult.com: Famous People With ADHD

ADD-ADHD-Treatments.com: Famous People With ADHD

YouTube.com: Famous People With ADD ADHD

Adult-Child-ADD-ADHD.com: Famous People With Adult – Child ADD – ADHD

Hallowellcenter.com: Famous People With ADD/ADHD

Lesson Tutor: 26 Positive Things About ADD and 46 Famous People

EverydayHealth.com: Celebrities With ADHD

Facebook.com: Famous People With ADD/ADHD

OrganizedWisdom.com: Celebrities And Stars With ADD/ADHD

IMDB.com: Celebrities With A History Of ADD/ADHD

KidTestedParentApproved.com: Famous People With ADD ADHD

WRCH.CBSLocal.com: Famous People with ADD/ADHD

ADDSuccess.co.uk: Famous People With ADD and Dyslexia

FamousADD.com: Famous People With ADD/ADHD

Psychcentral.com: Famous People With ADHD

Health.com: Celebrities With ADHD

Justine Ruotolo has been an ADD/Life Coach for over twenty years. A graduate of the Pepperdine University MFT program, her practice is located in Torrance, California, where she also serves on the board of CHADD (Children and Adults with ADD).

After being diagnosed with ADD at age 40, Justine started working on releasing her past and embracing her own creativity. Through her own struggle, she developed a self-awareness and was able to regulate her emotions, so much so that she was able to drastically reduce her ADD medication. Through this work, she was able to transform trauma into positive growth.

This personal transformation inspired her to share what she had learned so that others may uncover the gifts of ADD so often buried beneath its stigma and stereotypes. She leads a powerful support group for adults with ADD in the South Bay of California that started with four members and now has roughly thirty.

Justine also works with parents of ADD children, negotiating accommodations for their children including and assisting with 504 plans and IEP meetings. She also helps children and adolescents with organization, study skills, behavior and time management. Her work with adults includes emotional individuation, mindfulness and meditation.

Justine has an intense passion for helping children, adolescents, parents, adults and couples embrace their ADD and understand the gifts associated with their "Creative Mindset."

She can be reached at TheGiftofADD@MissADD.com.

Made in the USA
Middletown, DE
03 May 2017

Did you know that ADD is a gift?

The majority of the artists, innovators, creators and entrepreneurs of the world have ADD. This includes people like Steven Spielberg, Justin Timberlake, Richard Branson, Steve Jobs, Bill Gates, Picasso, Frank Lloyd Wright, Michael Phelps, Michael Jordan, John F. Kennedy, and Agatha Christie, to name a few. This book serves as a resource for the ADD population to see examples of successful ADD people—people who have overcome obstacles and achieved success in every field imaginable. It also includes case studies of clients Justine Ruotolo has worked with, highlighting the successes they were able to achieve once they embraced their ADD as a gift rather than an obstacle.

"Justine Ruotolo has helped many clients who have struggled for years with the symptoms of ADD and the negative view of themselves they internalized from childhood. Using her twenty years of experience, Justine not only teaches solution-focused techniques that effectively transform ADD behaviors, but she helps clients to see that their ADD is truly a gift. By compiling this book, Justine can now help many more children, teens and adults."

--Ellen Kimmel, LCSW.

"Justine gave me the tools and support to change my life-long ADD patterns. For the first time I became aware of what I was doing and why I was doing it. I finally understand that I do what I do not because I am lazy and incompetent, but because of my executive functioning. Justine made me feel that my ADD is a gift."

--Harry Davidow, MBA

Flying Chickadee

ISBN 9780615882116

90000

9 780615 882116